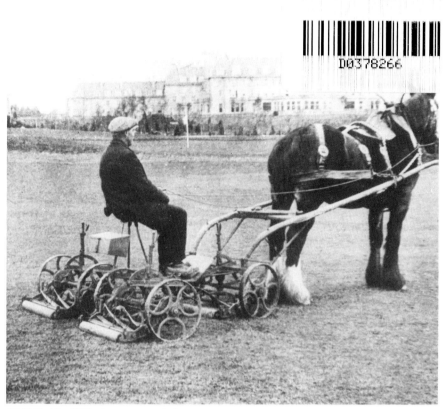

ABOVE: *The 1920s Ransomes triple horse gang units became typical of the period after their introduction following the First World War.*

FRONT COVER: *Ransomes, Sims and Jefferies Mark 8 24-inch (600 mm) lawnmower. This model was manufactured between 1936 and 1953 and was very advanced in design when introduced. A four-stroke Sturmey Archer engine powered the unit. Many Ransomes models were powered by this manufacturer's engine during the 1950s. Sturmey Archer is possibly better known for its three-speed cycle units.*

OLD LAWNMOWERS

David G. Halford

Shire Publications Ltd

CONTENTS

Published in 2008 by Shire Publications Ltd,
Midland House, West Way, Botley, Oxford OX2
0PH, UK. Website: www.shirebooks.co.uk

Copyright © 1982 by David G. Halford. First
published 1982, reprinted 1993, 1999 and 2008
(twice). Shire Album 91.
ISBN 978 0 85263 607 7.

Printed in Great Britain by Ashford Colour Press Ltd, Unit 600, Fareham Reach, Fareham Road,
Gosport, Hants PO13 0FW.

08/1/5

The Lawnrider, made by the British Anzani Engineering Company Ltd of Maidstone, is a ride-on
cylinder mower and was based on a design manufactured by E. F. Ranger (Ferring) Ltd, Littlehampton,
during the mid 1950s.

The first lawnmower manufactured by John Ferrabee of Stroud to the Edwin Budding patent of 1830. The grass box (d) consisted of a flat tray, while the small height-regulating roller (b) is situated behind the cylinder (c).

INVENTION OF THE LAWNMOWER

It was not until the introduction of grass-cutting machinery that large areas of grass were included in private gardens. The most rapid increase in the number of lawns followed the First World War when detached and semi-detached houses, each with a small garden, began to supersede terraced homes. Lawns required less time and effort than flowerbeds when the lawnmower had become a common piece of machinery. This change was responsible for the growth of an important industry. Cricket fields, bowling greens, golf courses, tennis courts, croquet lawns, football and hockey pitches shared the benefit and the games played on them improved through the provision of short grass.

The development from the scythe to the most modern of mowers has covered a period of 150 years and it is difficult to visualise what further improvement will take place.

A good gardener using a special scythe could produce a very good low-cut finish. Grass was easier to cut when it was wet with dew, late at night or early in the morning, as it stood well against the blade. Lawns were found only at stately homes and manor houses; public parks did not appear until the latter part of the nineteenth century when wealthy industrialists created recreational areas for the working population. Small cottage gardens were cultivated to produce as much food as possible.

The idea of a machine to cut grass was conceived at Stroud in Gloucestershire around 1830. A freelance engineer, Edwin Beard Budding, who was previously a carpenter at Chalford, worked for various local mill owners and the idea of cutting grass with a rotary (cylindrical) cutter probably came to him after seeing a rotary cutter designed to cut the nap off wool cloth at Brinscomb Mill.

Edwin Budding was thirty-five years old when he went into partnership with John Ferrabee, who had taken the lease on Thrupp Mill — a little way downstream from Brinscomb — and formed the Phoenix

Foundry in 1828. In the agreement of 18th May 1830 John Ferrabee paid for the cost of development, obtained letters patent and had the right to manufacture, sell and license other manufacturers to produce lawnmowers. The profits were to be divided and the agreement was bound to either party to the sum of £2,000. (The agreement is now housed in Stroud Museum.)

The patent of 25th October 1830 referred to 'a new combination and application of machinery for the purpose of cropping or shearing the vegetable surfaces of lawns, grass-plats, and pleasure grounds, constituting a machine which may be used with advantage instead of a scythe for that purpose'. After the technical details a summary is given and in conclusion states that 'grass growing in the shade, too weak to stand against the scythe to cut, may be cut by my machine as closely as required, and the eye will never be offended by those circular scars, inequalities and bare places so commonly made by the best mowers with the scythe, and which continues visible for

several days. Country gentlemen may find in using my machine themselves an amusing, useful and healthy exercise.' The process of cutting the grass has remained much the same.

One of the first Budding and Ferrabee lawnmowers was used at Regent's Park Zoological Gardens in 1831. The foreman, Mr Curtis, was entirely satisfied with the machine: 'it does as much work as six or eight men with scythes and brooms ... performing the whole so perfectly as not to leave a mark of any kind behind.'

The author of one of the first articles on lawnmowers to appear rejoiced that grass cutting could be done at a reasonable hour and lawn growing would be encouraged, and he had little doubt that the mower would soon be modified to be worked by ponies, donkeys or small steam engines. But it took a further ten years before a pony-powered machine came on the market and sixty years for a steam-powered lawnmower.

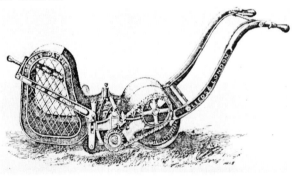

This 1859 Greens lawnmower established the form of future machines. The chain drive was a great step forward as it was much simpler and quieter than the normal gear drive. This model was called Silens Messor. It was manufactured in a number of sizes ranging from 14 inch (350 mm) in 2 inch steps to 24 inch (600 mm). Three donkey and pony machines were also offered, from 24 inch (600 mm) to 30 inch (750 mm).

BELOW: *This was the first design of lawnmower by Thomas Green of Leeds, in 1856. The machine was pulled and was available in three sizes: 16 inch (400 mm) at £6, 20 inch (500 mm) at £7, and 24 inch (600 mm) at £8.*

This photograph of a lawnmower in use at New College, Oxford, is thought to have been taken in the 1880s. The machine may have been manufactured by James Ferrabee at the Phoenix Foundry, Stroud, in the early 1860s. James was the son of John Ferrabee, manufacturer of the Budding machines.

EARLY LAWNMOWERS

A fault of the Ferrabee machine was that the small wooden roller was placed behind the cylinder and very close to the rear drive roller. The cylinder, or cutting unit, was difficult to control and was often forced into the ground, leaving an uneven height of cut. The simple drive clutch had to be held in position to obtain the drive. The gears were very crude at this period as machine-cut gears did not appear until some years later. The machine was made of cast iron.

The idea of mechanical grass cutting did not spread very rapidly. John Ferrabee had the right to issue licences to manufacturers and the firm of J. R. and A. Ransome of Ipswich, already well known for agricultural machinery, took up the first one, issued in 1832. Its grass-cutting division is now an extremely important part of Ransomes, Sims and Jefferies, still based in Ipswich, and is the largest manufacturer of grass-cutting equipment in Europe.

In 1841 W. F. Lindsay Carnegie persuaded a local engineer, Alexander Shanks of Arbroath, to construct a 27 inch (675

mm) wide mower for his 2½ acre (1 ha) lawn. They found that it could be pulled by a small pony without leaving permanent hoof marks on the grass and Carnegie was able to cut his lawn in two and a half hours. In 1842 Shanks registered the design of a machine that was 42 inches (1050 mm) wide and so the use of animal power was established. Horse machines continued to be made until 1939. This 1842 machine still had the small roller behind the cylinder but as the machine was 'pulled' it did not have the same tendency to dig into the ground.

In 1856 Alexander Shanks took out a further patent for a pulled machine which had one wheel in front and the drive roller, which supplied the power via gearing, at the rear. A grass box was fitted in front of the cylinder. This patent was taken out on 21st May and on 24th June Thomas Green of Leeds took out a patent for a machine that was virtually identical and was offered in various sizes. These machines were incredibly long and cumbersome but Shanks continued to manufacture this design for

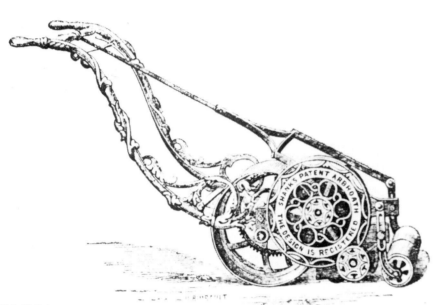

This 1862 lawnmower was produced by Alexander Shanks and Son of Arbroath and shows unusual cast iron handles for this two-person model. This machine was gear-driven.

some years and one can be seen in Arbroath Museum.

Thomas Green soon realised that the front wheel could be replaced by a small roller in front of the cylinder. James Ferrabee also moved the roller from behind the cylinder but later replaced it with two wheels and finally reverted to a roller, but in front. By 1862 his company was making eight models in various sizes up to 36 inches (900 mm) at prices varying between £4 10s and £20. He manufactured over five thousand machines but production ceased after 1863.

The drive to the cutting cylinder was to remain a problem for many years. In 1830 adequate machine tools were not available and all the early machines were driven by gears which were cast. The drive was taken from the rear roller shaft by means of a large gear that meshed with a smaller gear in front. This was fitted to the end of a shaft which ran across the machine and had a larger gear fitted on the other end to drive the cylinder cutter. This gearing was exposed on both sides of the machine. The drive to the rear roller shaft was obtained by using a sliding gear or dog which had to be held in position but automatically dis-

engaged when the machine was pulled backwards. The first mowers had only one drive rear roller which did not extend the full width of the machine and so only one clutch was required. Later machines, as they became wider, were fitted with two rollers and these required two clutch levers. Some of these early machines can be seen in Stroud Museum and the Science Museum, South Kensington.

In 1859 Green introduced a chain drive which ran on a gear which was machine-cut, not a sprocket. (This type of chain is now called a *transmission chain* and is like an endless flexible gear with the teeth on the inside.) The rear roller had an internal gear cut on the inside and this meshed with a small gear which had another gear on the short shaft which carried the chain.

Between the transmission and roller chain a block chain was used and this continued into the early 1900s. This chain looked strange as it ran on a sprocket which had half the usual number of teeth and the chain had solid sections between the open sections. It was used extensively by other lawnmower manufacturers, some of whom fitted two sprockets to the cylinder, one each end, so that the operator could turn the cylinder around when the cutting edge became blunt and the other edge of the blade could be used. Better machine tools, able to cut gears, were appearing towards the end of the nineteenth century and the roller chain used on the safety bicycle in the 1890s was adapted by manufacturers.

It was well into the 1900s before most manufacturers began to produce the drive on one side of the machine only. Before this it was common to find the gears covered by attractive castings, which had the advantage of keeping fingers out, but as most were open castings they did not keep out dirt. Early machines were very noisy and as late as 1897 many gardeners were not allowed to use their mowers early in the morning before everyone had woken. This problem was considerably reduced by the use of chains and the first chain-driven mower produced by Green in 1859 was named the Silens Messor.

In 1863 Barnard, Bishop and Barnard tried a friction drive in place of gears or early chains. They used India rubber covered wheels to replace the gears but there must have been problems with the rubber wheels slipping when wet. The machine would have been very quiet!

Over the years the clutches in the rear rollers were replaced by pawls, which were free to swing, and so two were fitted to each section. Pawls are still extensively used but are now enclosed and assisted by springs.

Around 1900 it was not uncommon for manufacturers to offer both gear and chain driven machines for the same price. One of the best known models offered in 1897 was Ransomes' Automaton, available as chain or gear drive, from the 10 inch (250 mm) at £3 10s to the 18 inch (450 mm) at £7 10s. Later the price of chains came down and chain-driven machines were often cheaper.

JP Engineering of Leicester, founded just after the First World War, produced a range of very popular chain-driven mowers. The chain ran inside the main

Ransomes, Sims and Jefferies Ltd of Ipswich introduced this Gear Automaton model in 1895 although the model name had been used by them for earlier machines. The gears were covered with a casting, but chain-driven models were not. This firm started manufacturing lawnmowers in 1832 to the Budding design but was then known as J. R. and A. Ransome.

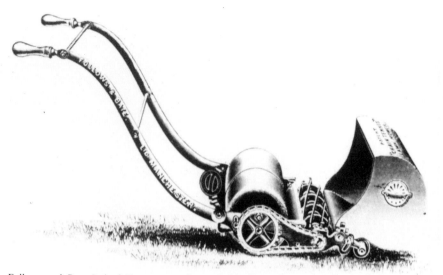

Follows and Bate Ltd of Gorton manufactured this Chain Tennis model in 1900 but they were better known for their side-wheel driven lawnmowers.

frame and was totally enclosed. The cylinder or cutting unit could be very easily and quickly removed for resharpening.

Externally the roller-drive lawnmower has changed little since about 1930.

Manufacturers soon produced machines with varying numbers of blades, the higher the number the better the quality of cut. Blades were attached at first with crimped wire, then with split pins, by rivets and finally by welding.

Because of the tendency for the grass to be thrown to one side of the grass box, a cylinder was developed in the 1890s with blades set in two directions so that the grass was thrown into both sides of the box, but this proved to be expensive and was dropped by the manufacturers. Later, however, JP used it for a time, as did the firm of Allet.

As the metal of the blades was not very good they soon became blunt so most manufacturers offered a handle with which to rotate the cylinder backwards. By applying 'flowers of emery' to the blades they were sharpened. This process is known as *back lapping* and is still extensively used in the United States.

The first grass boxes were flat trays but they took their present shape in the 1860s. Boxes were often constructed of metal with wooden sides and this reduced the noise.

Until 1939 most were fitted with cast iron handles for lifting.

Rear-roller springing was introduced by Shanks in 1895 and was designed to reduce the vibration caused by the uneven lawns of that period. It was fitted to their Caledonia model and their larger animal-powered machines. The idea was taken up by some other manufacturers but was confined to the larger models. As lawn surfaces improved springing became unnecessary.

Frames, handles and rear-drive rollers were all made of cast iron until after the First World War when JP Engineering started to produce mowers of cast aluminium. Other firms followed, using aluminium for chain cases and, at the same time, flat steel for handles and frames. Pressed steel was not used for frames until 1929 when H. C. Webb Ltd introduced their first model, called the De Luxe. Today mowers are a mixture of cast iron, aluminium, pressed and cut steel and plastic.

Catalogues published before the First World War and especially those of the late nineteenth century offered a large choice of makes and sizes. Whereas today nearly all hand mowers are of 12 inch (300 mm) cut, machines as small as 6 inches (150 mm) were made and sizes increased by 2 inch (50 mm) steps up to 20 inch (500 mm). The

TOP: *Shanks introduced springing to this chain-driven Caledonia model in 1895 to reduce the vibration caused by uneven lawns.*

ABOVE: *H. C. Webb Ltd of Birmingham commenced manufacturing lawnmowers in 1928 with the De Luxe, which was the first lawnmower to have the side frame made of pressed steel.*

RIGHT: *Qualcast Ltd, Derby, commenced production of the Panther in 1932 and this model became a best seller over the years. The Qualcast Company was originally known as the Derwent Iron Foundry (1920) Ltd but changed its title to its trade name in 1928. This advertisement, of 1956, claims over one million machines in use.*

9

range was also described by the type of power required: the smallest were referred to as ladies' models, followed by boys', man, man and boy, and finally two-man. Where two people were required one had to pull on a rope or, with the very early models, a metal handle. Models above 20 inch (500 mm) width were animal-powered.

Draught animals were fitted with leather boots, available in sizes for horse, pony and donkey, to minimise the damage to the lawns. This type of mower developed on the same lines as the hand machines but was larger and stronger. As there were fewer manufacturers in this field the range was smaller. Before 1900 the operator walked behind the machine but about that date seats were fitted in front of the handles so that the person could ride or walk. Eventually petrol-driven machines replaced horse-drawn mowers although there are still a few in use today.

The grass box was placed behind the animal's back feet, from which position it had to be emptied. A method had to be found of emptying the box without the operator leaving the reins or handles. The most common arrangement was called *side delivery* and consisted of a nearly square grass box, the side of which were replaced with hinged flaps. A board, which ran on rails, moved from one side of the box to the other, allowing the grass to fall out through the hinged flap. The board was moved sideways either by a long lever or by means of cables or chains with a pulley or sprocket attached to the handles.

Another solution was to have a chain that lifted the box up and tipped the grass behind the rear roller by means of a sprocket fitted on the handles.

Machine sizes depended on the type of animal power. Donkey mowers started at 22 inches (550 mm), pony mowers around 30 inches (750 mm) and horse machines around 36 inches (900 mm), but the wide machines of 42 inches (1050 mm) lost popularity over the years. John Crowley and Company Ltd of Sheffield, makers of the Invincible lawnmower, produced in 1894 a range of sizes for animals from the 24 inch (600 mm) with side delivery at £14 to the 42 inch (1050 mm) at £30, prices typical for this period.

Arundel Coulthard and Company Ltd of Preston were forced to look for new products to manufacture during the mid 1930s to keep the foundry busy. Lawnmowers were chosen and a range of hand and petrol powered models were produced over the years. This five-blade model was known as the 5-15. It looks rather similar to the Qualcast Panther.

JP Engineering Ltd of Leicester commenced manufacturing lawnmowers after the First World War. An engineer realised that there was a shortage of gardeners and there would be a market for high quality machines. This late 1930s powered lawnmower was fitted with a two-stroke engine and the only clutch was fitted in the rear roller. To protect people from the revolving cylinder, a flap was fitted which automatically covered it when the grass box was removed.

RIGHT: Horse boots were worn to reduce the damage to lawns. Various sizes were available to suit horses, ponies and donkeys. They were also made to measure. Measurements were taken by placing the hoof on a piece of paper and running a pencil around it.

BELOW: Thomas Green's Silens Messor 1928 pony and horse lawnmower. This model was chain-driven and the grass box emptied by rotating a shaft that ran across the machine and over the rear roller. The grass was tipped at the feet of the gardener. A seat could be supplied for him to sit on if the animal was experienced.

ABOVE: *Alexander Shanks's horse lawnmower of 1922. Like the Caledonia, it was fitted with rear-roller springing but was gear-driven. The grass box was rigid and was emptied by sweeping the grass cuttings to the side by means of a piece of wood that was propelled sideways by a handle situated high above the handles. This model was available in three sizes: 30 inch (750 mm) at £64 10s; 36 inch (900 mm) at £72; and 42 inch (1050 mm) at £77 10s.*

BELOW: *This Follows and Bate pony mower is gear-driven and is fitted with the simplest of grass-box emptying devices. The two sides of the box are joined together by rods and the grass is removed by pulling the sides outwards.*

Follows and Bate introduced the side-wheel lawnmower in 1869 with their Climax. It was available in four sizes from 6 inch (150 mm) to 10 inch (250 mm) and with its much lower production costs it became available to a far wider section of the population. This is a 6 inch model.

SIDE-WHEEL LAWNMOWERS

A roller fitted in front of the cylinder pressed long grass down before it was cut. In 1869 Follows and Bate of Gorton, near Manchester, took out an important patent which led to a range of new designs in which the small front roller was transferred to the rear of the machine and the driving roller was split into two sections and was moved to the sides of the cylinder to become wheels. The drive to the cylinder was obtained directly from the wheels by having a gear on each end of the cylinder which meshed with an internal gear on the inside of the wheel rim. A ratchet was fitted to each end of the cylinder to enable the two wheels to rotate at different speeds but it took some years before this drive was perfected.

The grass box could be fitted either at the rear of the machine or at the front with the use of a front delivery plate. This was often an extra cost, as was the box. A later model from Follows and Bate, called the Speedwell, had a canvas grass box at the rear.

Side-wheel machines became very popular, mainly because of their lower price.

The Gripper, made by Alex C. Harris of Leicester, sold at 10s 6d in 1909. Most of the competitors cost at least a pound more.

This style of machine suited the American market and it was not long before American firms were manufacturing and exporting them. The American mowers were mostly cheaper than the British but were very plain, having no name or model number cast into the wheels, and no maker's badge attached to the base of the wooden T handle which was a distinct feature of most side-wheel machines.

When long grass was being cut the rear roller lifted up and a front-mounted grass box tended to hit the ground and come off, spilling its contents. The American manufacturers corrected this by adding a gear between the wheels and the cylinder. This type of machine is easily identifiable because it is somewhat longer than the normal side-wheel machine.

John Post Lawrence, of Somerset, became the British agent of Lloyd, Supplee and Walton, American manufacturers of the Pennsylvania range of mowers, and in 1879 he founded Lloyd Lawrence and

The Follows and Bate Speedwell (1900) had a canvas grass box at the rear. A grass box could be fitted at the front if a grass deflector plate was used.

BELOW: *Lloyds and Company (Letchworth) Ltd imported Pennsylvania lawnmowers which were manufactured by the Supplee Hardware Company, Philadelphia, USA, but later Lloyds manufactured them in Britain. This design differed from the majority of side-wheel models in that it had an extra gear between the wheels and the cylinder which kept the rear roller in contact with the ground when long grass was being cut.*

This 1939 Ransomes Leo Bank Cutter was a standard side-wheel mower fitted with an extra-long handle.

Company, importing five sizes of machine from 10 inch (250 mm) to 18 inch (450 mm). These machines cost virtually the same as those of Follows and Bate but their design was better. In 1920 the firm became Lloyds and Company (Letchworth) Ltd and their premises, the Pennsylvania Works, are still in Letchworth. In 1934 economic circumstances obliged them to stop importing mowers and to manufacture their own machines. These were identical in design and had the letters 'PQ' (Pennsylvania quality) cast into the frames. They continued to produce machines based on this layout but because of the high demand for the larger sizes they stopped making hand machines and concentrated on professional types. They did, however, produce some interesting machines for cutting the grass up against buildings and walls. One had a flat side and only one driving wheel, together with a small wheel on the inside to support the front of the machine. Another machine had a cone-shaped cutting cylinder with the wider end cutting close to the wall. The side plate was also angled and this machine cut virtually right up to the wall.

As the side-wheel drive mower could not cut up to the edge of the lawn some manufacturers offered a small wheel which could be attached to the front of the machine, in front of the cylinder, to support the machine when one wheel was over the edge.

From about 1900 until the Second World War side-wheel machines were often available with an extra long wooden handle for use on banks. This enabled the gardener to stand at the top or bottom of the slope to operate the mower.

After the Second World War hundreds of thousands of houses with their own gardens were built and the market for domestic lawnmowers grew enormously. A vast range of side-wheel machines was available until the introduction during the 1970s of cheap electrically powered mowers. These soon superseded the side-wheel and rear-roller drive hand models.

Typical prices of Follows and Bate side-wheel machines in 1903 were: Runaway, 9 inch (230 mm), £1 14s to 19 inch (480 mm) £3 16s 6d; and Speedwell, 7 inch (180 mm) £1 1s 9d to 11 inch (280 mm), fitted with extra long handles for mowing banks, £1 14s 6d.

In 1900 Alexander Shanks produced a steam-powered lawnmower where the driver sat on the machine but this was changed in 1902 and it then became very similar to the Leyland.

STEAM-POWERED LAWNMOWERS

Not until over sixty years after the invention of the lawnmower was a steam engine fitted to one. Elias Sumner and his two sons, James and William, of Leyland, Lancashire, were blacksmiths and often had to work away from home. This travelling prompted James, who had experimented with steam power, to produce a steam-powered tricycle. He was once fined one shilling for going too fast! Some time later the sons were presented with an old lawnmower. The twin-cylinder steam engine from the tricycle was mounted on top of this and produced the first powered mower. In 1893 James took out a patent for 'Improvement in steam boilers applicable for use in connection with lawnmowers'. Steam engines of this period were usually coal-fired but the Sumner machine was different and used petroleum or paraffin oil, carried in a tank in the top of the chimney. The model advertised initially had a tall slender boiler and chimney, but there is little evidence that it was actually produced.

In 1894 the boiler was enlarged, with a corresponding shortening of the chimney, and in 1895 the fuel was transferred to a

16

container alongside the water reservoir just behind the boiler. A hand pump was incorporated to pressurise the tank initially, and when steam was raised, in ten minutes, the machine took over the job of maintaining pressure. This improvement seems to have worked and it became fairly popular. At first the machines seem to have been sold by the Stott Fertiliser and Insecticide Company of Manchester but as they became more popular Sumners took over the sales themselves. In 1895 the company changed its title to the Leyland Steam Motor Company, now BL. One of their machines can be seen in the Museum of English Rural Life, University of Reading.

Two sizes were offered in 1897: a 25 inch (525 mm) machine which sold for £60, and a 30 inch (750 mm) for £90. The operator walked behind the machine with a large steam regulator in front. It was not easy to control or turn in tight corners as it travelled at 4 miles (6 km) per hour and weighed over a ton. It was noisy and was not immediately successful.

About this time the petrol engine was gaining popularity and in 1896 Mr W. J. Stephenson-Peach, MIME, of Askew Hill, Burton upon Trent, Professor of Engineering to Repton School and Cheltenham College, designed and produced steam-powered, mains electrical and petrol-powered lawnmowers. The operator of the steam-powered model sat on a seat on the front of the machine.

In 1900 Alexander Shanks also made a steam-powered mower with a rear seat. It was steered by controlling an additional small roller at the back. This design was changed in 1903 to a similar layout to the Sumner with the operator walking behind. In 1902 Thomas Green produced another ride-on steam machine but the driver sat in front of the boiler, steering in the same manner as the 1900 Shanks.

Steam mowers arrived too late, however, because in 1902 Ransomes introduced a petrol-driven mower.

James Sumner of Leyland produced the first steam-powered lawnmower in 1892. It was modified in 1895 but still weighed about 1½ tons.

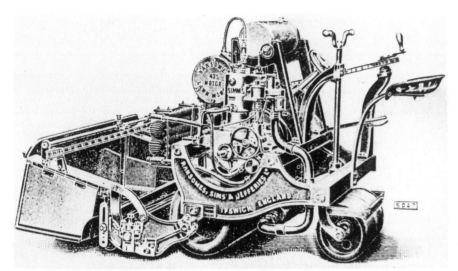

ABOVE: *Ransomes' petrol-powered lawnmower was the first to be sold. It was 42 inches (1050 mm) wide and powered by a German 6 horsepower (4.5 kW) Simms engine. It still retained the same system of grass-box emptying as the animal-powered models.*

BELOW: *A 1929 Greens 42 inch (1050 mm) water-cooled petrol-powered lawnmower weighed 1 ton and sold for £325. Over the years, from the introduction of this machine in 1902, the main changes were to cover the engine and improve the appearance.*

The Auto-Mower Engineering Company Ltd, Bath, manufactured lawnmowers from the mid 1920s until the mid 1930s.

PETROL-ENGINED LAWNMOWERS

Although Stephenson-Peach had designed a petrol-driven mower in 1896 it seems unlikely that his was the first as Messrs Grimsley manufactured petrol-driven machines in 1897. Ransomes produced the first commercial machine in 1902, after experiments carried out by J. E. Ransome. It had a cutting width of 42 inches (1050 mm) and was powered by a Simms 6 horsepower (4.5 kW) four-stroke engine that was water-cooled. It was steered by a small roller under the seat at the rear of the machine. The first machine was sold to Mr Prescott Westcar of Herne Bay and the second to Cadbury Brothers for their Bournville sports ground.

In 1903 Greens and Ransomes each produced a 24 inch (600 mm) mower with a $2\frac{3}{4}$ horsepower (2.1 kW) water-cooled engine with fan, priced £70. Although offered for sale, the Greens machine was only experimental and in the trial organised that year at the Hanger Hill Golf Club, Ealing, the Royal Agricultural Society reported that the two machines were 'very similar . . . The rollers of Messrs Ransomes' machine were driven through a differential gear, whereas those of Messrs Green and Son were fitted with two clutches, by which either roller at option, or both, could be made drivers . . . when it came to a test for handiness, the differential drive of Messrs Ransomes' machine showed to great advantage.'

The superiority of the petrol engine over the steam engine was proved when Ran-

ABOVE: *This 1907 Ransomes 24 inch (600 mm) motor mower is also powered by a Simms engine but was air-cooled. It has a chain drive and the grass box is fitted with side delivery emptying.*

BELOW: *Greens' 1929 light motor lawnmower, which was air-cooled, was available in either 16 or 20 inch (400 or 500 mm) width of cut. The 16 inch was powered by a $1\frac{3}{4}$ horsepower (13 kW) engine and sold for £37 10s, while the 20 inch was powered by a $2\frac{1}{2}$ horsepower (1.9 kW) engine and sold for £52. They weighed about 2 hundredweights (100 kg).*

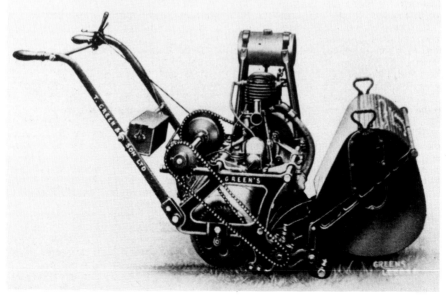

*The first of a long range of mowers powered by Charles H. Pugh Ltd, of Birmingham was this 1926
Atco Standard.*

somes sent their third machine, a 20 inch
(500 mm), to Eaton Hall near Chester to
compete against the Leyland steam mower.
The success of Ransomes' machine was
such that King Edward VII ordered a
demonstration to be carried out in the
grounds of Buckingham Palace and the
short era of the steam mower was over.

The original Ransome was a 42 inch
(1050 mm) machine with a similar layout
to the first Shanks steam machine – a cast
iron roller placed behind the cylinder which
propelled the machine, steered by a smaller
roller at the rear. The operator sat above
this with the engine in front. Such a
machine was very heavy but this was an
advantage as lawns were often uneven at
that period. They retained the side delivery
method of emptying the grass box and a
handle was provided close to the seat with
either chain or cable mechanism. The
engines were water-cooled until 1939 and
Ransomes continued to produce them for a
few years after the war.

The main improvements were in the
engines fitted, which, as they developed,
were covered over with a hinged bonnet as
on cars. Over the years this type of
machine has rendered great service to
cricket clubs not only in mowing the grass
but also in rolling the wicket.

There were only three main manufacturers of this type of machine: Greens,
Shanks and Ransomes. In 1925 typical
prices for Shanks were: 42 inch (1050
mm), £335; 35 inch (900 mm), £280.

The first hand machines were still fairly
heavy; even one with a cut of 24 inches
(600 mm) weighed a few hundredweight,
and they still retained side emptying grass
boxes.

Between the two world wars new
manufacturers entered the field, such as
Dennis Brothers of Guildford, JP Engineering of Leicester, Charles H. Pugh of Birmingham (Atco lawnmowers) and
Qualcast of Derby.

The Atco (from the Atlas Chain Company) was chain-driven, powered by a
Villiers engine with a 'Senspray' carburet-
tor. These 22 inch (550 mm) mowers were
put on the market in 1921/2, direct to the

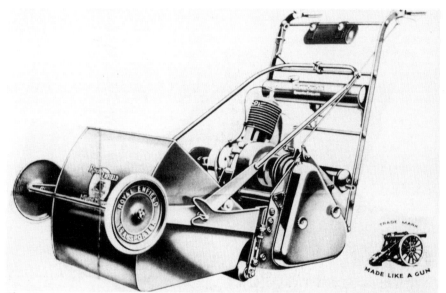

The 1936 20 inch (500 mm) Royal Enfield lawnmower sold for £45. To help in the emptying of the detachable grass box, it was fitted with wheels and a handle. The Enfield Cycle Company produced a range of five models during the 1930s.

public, and there are some of these early machines still cutting grass today. Atco set up service branches throughout Britain, the only firm to do this. Their first model was called the Standard and was made in a wide range of sizes. It had malleable cast iron sides, which, in the first year, were produced for them by Qualcast. Steel was used for the Deluxe model in 1930 and the 22 inch (550 mm) Standard model cost £75 when introduced but during the following years the price fell and in 1935 two ranges of machines, lightweight and middleweight, were launched, the cheaper being below £15.

The Dennis machine of 1921 was unsuccessful but the 1922 model became a great success. They fitted a number of different makes of engine before settling on a Blackburn, which they manufactured. This engine, except for a few modifications, was retained until Dennis ceased production about 1970. The name remained but the mowers were manufactured by the Dennis Godstone Engineering Company until 1981. Dennis did not enter the small domestic market but specialised in 30 inch (750 mm) machines. One unusual feature was the grass box, which could be

removed and placed upside down over the engine to keep off the rain when not in use. It was not unusual for manufacturers to offer lawnmower garages, low corrugated steel horseshoe-shaped structures, too low to walk into.

JP Engineering's first petrol-powered machines had a water-cooled engine that could be removed and used for other purposes.

The three main manufacturers offered a wide range of models, often fitting air-cooled motorcycle engines. Later Villiers, JAP or BSA makes were fitted and Ransomes used Sturmey Archer engines for some time. Today several foreign makes are also popular. Shanks ran into difficulties and turned to manufacturing gang units for Atco. They finally ceased production about 1970. Greens also had troubles and the lawnmower side was purchased by Hawker Siddeley in the 1960s and finally closed down. It has, however, been revived by Reekie Engineering of Arbroath, maintaining lawnmower manufacture in that town. It was started there by Shanks in 1841. Ransomes are still producing machines and have done so since 1832.

ABOVE: *Dennis Brothers of Guildford, well known for their lorries, started manufacturing lawnmowers in the early 1920s and this 1928 30 inch (750 mm) model sold for £90.*

BELOW: *This 1946 Qualcast Sixteen was one of the first petrol-powered lawnmowers manufactured by the firm, which was better known for its hand models.*

Several engineering firms, especially during the depression of the 1930s, manufactured mowers to keep their work force busy. Some of the better known were the Enfield Cycle Company, Redditch; Carrick and Ritchie Ltd, Edinburgh; Auto-Mower Engineering, Bath; and Arundel Coulthard and Company Ltd, Preston.

Larger engines were usually four-stroke and lubrication was often of the 'drip feed' type where the oil was allowed to drip from a tank through a sight glass into the engine. The oil was burnt and the rate of drip was controlled to produce a haze at the exhaust pipe. By the mid 1930s engines had a pump which delivered the correct amount of oil regardless of engine speed. Splash lubrication was being fitted to some American engines before the Second World War and was later taken up by British engine manufacturers and is the system that is still used today. Dennis Brothers had a forced feed lubrication system, right from the fitting of the Blackburn engine, and the oil was pumped around the engine as it is in motor cars, an extremely efficient method.

Two-stroke engines became popular after the First World War for use on the smaller domestic machines but, with the introduction of the very reliable small splash-lubricated four-stroke engine by Villiers in the 1950s, this type of engine was phased out. However, two-stroke engines are now fitted to rotary mowers, especially those of the hover (Flymo) type.

Nearly all the engines were air-cooled but some of the early ones had a propeller-type fan. In the late 1930s the fan was incorporated into the flywheel of the engine and a cowling fitted to direct the air across the cylinder head.

Ransomes were the first to fit a multi-cylinder water-cooled car engine (a Ford) to their machines in the 1950s and this was followed by Allet of Stamford with a Reliant engine. This trend has been copied by other manufacturers of large grass-cutting equipment.

Nearly all the early machines had a starting handle until after the Second World War. Later *kick starts* were fitted, followed by the *recoil start*. An increasing number of engines are being fitted with electric starters.

A two-stroke engine has to be turned over quite fast to get it to fire and this was achieved by using a rope wrapped around a pulley on the end of the flywheel. As it has to run at fairly high engine speeds to develop its power, an intermediate chain reduction was fitted between the engine and the clutch. This layout enabled a starting handle to be fitted on the clutch shaft and so increase the speed. Where the clutch was on the end of the crankshaft an epicyclic clutch was fitted to obtain the necessary speed reduction and a separate chain drive was fitted to start the machine. By 1950 nearly all machines had this arrangement and the necessary reduction was obtained within the chain or gear case on the side of the machine.

Although it was possible to disengage the cylinder drive on some machines in the period between the wars most manufacturers offered mower transporters of one form or another. On all Dennis mowers the engine could be disengaged from the driving rollers and the cutting cylinder could be rotated alone, a great advantage when cutting small and awkward areas.

After the Second World War H. C. Webb started fitting petrol engines to their range of hand machines and still produce both hand and powered machines but mainly for the domestic market.

In 1930 Qualcast Derby produced their first mower, the Major, a rear-roller drive hand machine. It was not a success but the Panther of 1931 proved extremely popular. With various modifications and well over a million machines sold, it is still in production, which must surely be a record. One of their first petrol-powered machines appeared just before 1939 and was called the Sixteen. Later a very small two-stroke engine was fitted to the Panther CD model to power the cylinder only, the machine being pushed. Today Qualcast make electric-powered models also. Follows and Bate were taken over by Qualcast in 1938 and Folbate machines remained in production for many years.

In 1954 Suffolk Iron Foundry (1920) Ltd, Stowmarket, produced the Suffolk Colt and Suffolk Punch machines, which remain extremely popular. An engine production line was added to the factory to produce a 75 cc four-stroke engine to power the Colt. The Punch was powered by a 95 cc version and in 1980 a 95 cc

During the early 1920s lawnmower pushers were offered to the public to motorise their hand-pushed machines. This one was manufactured by W. Edgecumbe Rendle and Company Ltd and known as the Rendle Pusher.

aluminium engine was introduced for all the firm's models. In 1958 the company became part of the Qualcast Group, now the Birmid Qualcast Group of Companies, which also includes Atco. Arundel Coulthard, manufacturers of the Presto range, were also acquired and closed down.

About 1920 a method was sought of converting old hand machines to powered ones by making a *mower pusher,* a roller with an engine on top that was attached to the rear of the mower by means of a thick steel pin. Longer handles were fitted to the mower to allow for the additional length. The Rendle, manufactured by W. Edgecumbe Rendle and Company Ltd of London, was such a model and there were other makes available between the wars.

Some of the manufacturers of the large machines offered a trailing seat which was attached at the rear of the machine and this enabled the operator either to ride or to walk.

GANG MOWERS

Mr Worthington of Shawnee, USA, was the first manufacturer of gang units in 1919. His company was ultimately taken over by the Jacobsen Corporation but his name is still cast on to the frames of their gang units.

The Follows and Bate Anglo-American side-wheel machine of 1870, pulled by a pony, had the layout of a modern wheeled and propelled gang unit but was used only as a single unit.

The First World War delayed the introduction in England of multiple cutting units until 1920. They followed the American idea of side-wheel drive machines but as there was some resistance to this type in England most manufacturers produced both side-wheel and rear-roller drive types. The latter have been discontinued for a great many years, except by Allet of Stamford, who produced a petrol-driven rear-roller drive mower in 1965. They have now added a triple rear-roller drive gang mower to their range, giving a greater number of cuts per metre than can be achieved with the standard gang unit for areas that require a very high quality finish.

Side-wheel gang units have not changed very much except within the gear boxes, which have altered from chain drive to gear drive. The speed of operation has increased greatly, especially with the Lloyds Leda units.

During the 1930s old motorcars were

modified to draw gang units. Changes were made to the final drive to reduce the forward speed. The bodywork behind the dashboard was removed and a new body, looking like an open-fronted wooden shed on wheels, was often built to provide a load-carrying area that could be tipped. With the increase of power, five-unit machines appeared. Towards the end of the 1930s the agricultural tractor began to be used.

Three or more units are too wide for roads in their cutting position. Triple gang units may be pulled in tandem from site to site but the large five-gang units cannot be. These are moved on specially constructed trailers, drawn by a tractor or Land Rover, which allow easy loading and unloading on site, the units then being recoupled. Two types of special gang carriers are now available: on one type each unit is carried on an arm which can be lifted hydraulically and mounted on a trailer. On the other, an American design, the carriers are mounted on a lorry chassis.

As gang units received the power to turn their cutters from metal or pneumatic wheels placed either side of the machine, which were liable to slip on wet grass, Ransomes introduced cutters powered by hydraulic motors, one to each unit. The Hydraulic 5/7, of 1968, has five or seven units, each hydraulically powered, mounted around a tractor. It was the first with this drive method and is capable of cutting 5 acres (3.5 ha) in an hour at 5 miles per hour (8 km/h) with seven units. As the tractor cannot be used for any other work this type is used mostly by public authorities. For smaller users Ransomes introduced a mounted three-unit machine in 1977 and a mounted five-unit mower in 1978 which can be separated from the tractor. The units are lifted clear of the ground by the trac-

LEFT: *The 1922 Shanks 'Triumph' horse mower was typical of mowers that were used to cut sports areas before the advent of gang units. This 36 inch (900 mm) model was sold for £68 10s.*

BELOW: *A photograph showing a 1939 set of Ransomes gang units working on Oxford Airport.*

These 1926 Shanks triple gang units show how the rear roller has been replaced with two wheels set inside the frame.

tor's own hydraulics,which can also lift agricultural implements. Ransomes have been in the forefront of the development of hydraulically powered cutters and are Europe's largest industrial grass cutting machinery manufacturers and the third largest in the world.

Reekie of Arbroath, who took over the Greens name and designs, still produce the wheel-propelled types and hydraulically powered gang units. Lloyds manufacture their popular high-speed Leda gang units.

Gang units powered by the tractor's engine, by means of a shaft, were first used in 1977 by Sisis Ltd of Macclesfield.The cutters are mounted around a frame having two wheels at the rear and pulled like a trailer. There are three- or five-unit machines. Now the trend is for hydraulically- or belt-driven units mounted around the tractor or trailer.

The Shanks roller triple gang mower of 1937 shows that there was a demand for a rear roller drive mower for the finer cutting of turf. By this time gang units were being pulled by tractors or converted cars.

PETROL-POWERED SIDE-WHEEL MOWERS

The British-manufactured Pennsylvania, introduced in the 1930s and produced by Lloyds, had a clutch system that enabled the drive to be disengaged from either wheel so that the machine could be turned and steered by its own power, an arrangement still used on their current model. The cutting cylinder is in front of the cut-regulating roller, enabling the machine to cut longer and rougher grass.

Atco produced side-wheel powered machines with various engines. Their latest model is known as the Toughcut.

Ransomes made the small Antelope for the domestic market but have now concentrated on larger machines, starting with their Vergecutter in the 1950s. This had the drive wheels at the rear and castor wheels fitted on either side of the machine at the front. Their popular Multimower of 1959 was longer, more manoeuvrable and had a choice of cylindrical or rotary cutting action. It is used extensively for cutting grass around housing estates.

TRIPLE MOWERS

A triple mower has three cutting units, of various widths, mounted on a chassis, and the operator rides. The cylinders are powered by the engine and most are steered from the rear wheels, making them highly manoeuvrable.

In 1959 the Ransomes-Sisis Auto-Triple was the first British machine to have powered cylinders. It consisted of a small two-wheeled trailer with three cutting cylinders powered by an engine mounted on the trailer. The trailer was pulled by an Aero-main unit and the operator sat on the seat just in front of the engine on the trailer.

In 1963 Ransomes introduced the Motor Triple, which had two cutting cylinders in front of two front driving wheels, and the third under the machine in front of the rear steering wheels. This novel layout not only cuts the grass before it is rolled down by the wheels but it also gives an extremely tight turning circle — very useful for cutting around trees.

The Horwool triple machine of 1966 is based on a very small tractor with two cutting cylinders behind two front steering wheels and a third cylinder placed behind the rear driving wheels, very similar to a range of American machines. Nickerson Turfmaster Company Ltd took over the company in April 1977 and extended the range of widths of cut. It is not as manoeuvrable as a rear steered machine but the tractor can be used for other operations.

In 1977 Ransomes changed to fully hydraulic drive to both the cutters and the drive wheels for the Motor 5/3. Powered by a Ford four-cylinder water-cooled industrial engine, it has rear-wheel steering manoeuvrability and is available with three or five units.

The Lawnrider manufactured by the British Anzani Engineering Company from 1958 until 1968 was based on a design produced by E. F. Ranger (Ferring) Ltd, Littlehampton, known as the Easymow. It had a belt-driven single cutting cylinder with the engine mounted over a single drive roller situated behind the cylinder. The operator sat over the rear roller and steered the front half.

ELECTRICALLY POWERED MOWERS

The sales of the 1896 electric mower of W. J. Stephenson-Peach must have been very small as few houses would have had the necessary electrical supply. Even in the 1930s this type was not popular when it was reintroduced. But in 1959 when H. C. Webb fitted a 12 volt battery to their machines they started the era of battery mowers. The advantage of not having to start a petrol engine was a great boon, but they were not used professionally because of the limited amount of work that can be done between rechargings.

About 1950, as mentioned previously,

This 1937 Lloyds Penn-sylvania was designed to cut long grass and is a petrol-powered side-wheel machine.

The 1947 Lloyds Pegasus. This was introduced before the Second World War for the cutting of fine turf areas. The engine powered the cylinder only and the machine was very light.

Qualcast had fitted a small two-stroke engine to their CD model Panther, which powered the cylinder only. This idea was extended to the Electric Panther and finally to the Concorde – a very lightweight machine designed for the small garden.

Qualcast have produced over two million machines of this model.

Recently electrical rotary mowers have taken an ever increasing share of the market.

FINE GRASS-CUTTING MACHINES

Most people see really fine turf only on golf courses and bowling greens, where the grass has to be cut very short, to a height of only 3/16 inch (5 mm), with a high quality of finish for the ball to run true. Fine turf machines require more blades on the cylinder – ten or twelve blades compared with the average of six for domestic lawns – giving well over 125 cuts per metre.

The bottom blade must be thinner than the grass height required and the width of the machine is limited to about 20 inches (500 mm). This width is necessary to prevent the machine from removing all the grass and leaving brown areas, known as scalping. Golf courses and bowling greens are cut each day or every other day to remove just sufficient grass to maintain the finish.

For this specialised and limited use there have been fewer models produced. Early motor mowers were far too heavy and large so hand rear-roller machines were used. The most popular were Greens' Silens Messor De Luxe, Shanks' Golf Lynx and Ransomes' Certies. These machines were all gear-driven and were about 18 inches (450 mm) wide, much wider than the average hand machines. Greenkeepers were reluctant to change from hand machines so the change was slow.

In the late 1930s Lloyds introduced the Pegasus, a lightweight machine with a petrol engine powering the cylinder only. After the Second World War all the manufacturers were producing similar machines but during the 1950s the power was extended to the rear roller and at the same time Ransomes introduced the Bowlic electric-powered model, but it did not become popular. Atco produced a 20 inch (500 mm) Special and Lloyds their Paladin.

Transporting wheels were fitted for moving the machines between greens with the cutting mechanism well clear of the ground.

About 1970, Hayter, better known for their rotary mowers, introduced their Ambassador. Today the market is dominated by Ransomes with their Auto Certies, but Lloyds, Atco and Hayter are still active.

During the 1930s Ransomes introduced the Overgreen, a petrol engine powering two large pneumatic-tyred wheels which pulled three hand Certies units minus their handles, with the operator walking behind.

Much later Shanks produced a similar machine using their Gold Lynx units.

In the 1970s Ransomes imported from America the Hann Tournament Triplex, which, with many modifications, they later began to manufacture. It was renamed the Triplex 171 in 1980. This machine has hydrostatic transmission to the rear wheels. This is a variable displacement oil pump driving a fixed displacement motor and gives infinite variable forward and reverse gears and also incorporates the clutch. A Bowden cable (a flexible multi-strand cable) drives the cutting cylinders mounted in front and to the side of the twin front wheels. Their use is usually limited to golf greens because of their size and cost. Such is the area of a medium-sized golf course that a machine of this type will cover 1,000 miles (1600 km) per year cutting the greens only.

Machines for fine turf became available in the late 1980s with a scarafier between the cylinder and front roller. This concept is not new as Atco fitted a somewhat cruder version in the 1920s which they called a 'turf cultivator'. This range of machines has increased considerably, with hydraulic drive to the cylinders.

RIGHT: Vivian Lloyd and Company Ltd, London, manufactured rotary mowers during the early 1950s. This machine is completely unguarded, unlike the Hayter models of the same period.
BELOW: The 1955 Lloyds New Era fine turf mower competed with Greens' S-M Deluxe, Ransomes' Certies and Shanks' Lynx for mowing golf and bowling greens.

The Ransomes Overgreen consisted of a power unit that pulled and pushed three hand Certies units. It was used to cut golf greens before the Second World War and for a number of years afterwards.

ROTARY LAWNMOWERS

The rotary mower could not be developed until engines were small and powerful enough to rotate the blades at a sufficiently high speed to cut grass — 170 miles per hour (270 km/h) at the tip.

An attempt at rotary cutting that introduced a fixed disc with a series of slots cut into the front of it was made in 1874. The cutting was achieved by a blade which rotated above the fixed disc by means of a belt drive from the handle of the machine. The operator had to push the machine forward and at the same time turn the handle for the drive to the cutter. There is no evidence that this design was ever put into production.

In the 1930s Power Specialities Ltd, of Slough, introduced a petrol-powered rotary mower. This firm was taken over by J. E. Shay Ltd, of Basingstoke, in the late 1940s. The Shay Rotoscythe was very popular before and after the war. This firm was taken over by Wolseley Engineering in the early 1960s but rotary mowers are now produced by Hayter, Mountfield, Atco, Westwood, Landmaster and others. Firms mainly specialise in either the domestic or the professional market. Many rotary mowers, especially for domestic use, have a vertical crankshaft engine with the cutter attached directly to the shaft but the majority of cylinder mowers use horizontal crankshaft engines.

Flymo Ltd, part of Electrolux, introduced the first hover mower in 1966. Since their patent expired in the late 1970s other manufacturers have moved into this field.

A mains electrical rotary mower produced by Power Specialities Ltd over fifty years ago can be seen in the Halford Collection at Trerice Manor. A high proportion of the domestic grass cutters in use today are mains electric rotary types produced by Qualcast, Flymo, Wolf and Black & Decker.

On some rotary mowers the operator sits on the machine and many have the cutter mounted between the front and rear wheels of a mini tractor. Most of these are imported but the main British manufacturer in this field is Westwood.

Another development of the rotary mower since 1977 is the mono-nylon filament, which, when rotated at high speed, cuts the grass. As the nylon wears, more has to be fed out of a coil to maintain its correct length. Some models have the cutting deck 'out-front' with the operator seated over the drive wheels and the engine behind. They are fitted with hydrostatic transmission and rear wheel steering. Many have grass collection devices.

31

The Allen Scythe was introduced in the late 1930s for cutting long grass. It was manufactured in Oxford and was used extensively in orchards and poultry runs.

RECIPROCATING KNIFE MOWERS

The reciprocating knife mower has been extensively used in agriculture for grass and corn cutting since the nineteenth century. Initially horse-drawn, it consisted of a row of fixed fingers with a number of sharp knives moving backward and forward across the fingers as the machine was pulled forward, the width of cut being about 5 feet (1550 mm). Horticultural models were smaller, with a width of cut of 3 feet (900 mm). The best known is the Allen Scythe which appeared before the Second World War and remained in production until the mid 1970s. This model was self-propelled, but Lloyds and Atco produced machines with an engine powering the cutting mechanism only. The machine, supported on one large wheel, had to be pushed. Just before the war Atco reduced the size of the wheel and in the 1950s added another wheel and made the machine self-propelled. Lloyds also altered their machine by placing a wheel at either end of the cutting mechanism but both Lloyds and Atco had ceased production by 1960.

PLACES TO VISIT

Museum displays may be altered and readers are advised to telephone before visiting to check that relevant items are on show, as well as to find out times of opening.

Arbroath Signal Tower Museum, Ladyloan, Arbroath DD11 1PU. Telephone: 01241 875598. Website: www.angus.gov.uk/history/museums

Bicton Park Gardens (Countryside Museum), East Budleigh, Budleigh Salterton, Devon EX9 7BJ. Telephone: 01395 568465. Website: www.bictongardens.co.uk

British Lawnmower Museum, 106-114 Shakespeare Street, Southport PR8 5AJ. Telephone: 01704 501336. Website: www.lawnmowerworld.co.uk

Milton Keynes Museum, McConnell Drive, Wolverton, Milton Keynes MK12 5EL. Telephone: 01908 316222.The museum also provides a base for the **Old Lawnmower Club**; details from www.oldlawnmowerclub.co.uk

Museum of English Rural Life, The University, Redlands Road, Reading, Berkshire RG1 5EX. Telephone: 0118 378 8660. Website: www.reading.ac.uk/Instits/im

Museum of Garden History, Lambeth Palace Road, London SE1 7LB. Telephone: 0207 401 8865. Website: www.museumgardenhistory.org

The Museum in the Park, Stroud District Museum Service, Stratford Park, Stroud, Gloucestershire GL5 4AF. Telephone: 01453 763394. Website: www.stroud.gov.uk

Trerice, Kestle Mill, Newquay, Cornwall TR8 4PG. Telephone: 01637 875404. Website: www.nationaltrust.org.uk A permanent exhibition of British-manufactured grass-cutting machinery, based on the Halford Collection, was opened in 1981 to celebrate 150 years of the use of the lawnmower.